T0208139

Touching the Edge

Touching the Edge

*Dharma Devotions
from the
Hummingbird
Sangha*

MICHAEL McCLURE

SHAMBHALA
Boston & London
1999

Shambhala Publications, Inc.
Horticultural Hall
300 Massachusetts Avenue
Boston, Massachusetts 02115
http://www.shambhala.com

©1999 by Michael McClure

All rights reserved. No part of this book may be
reproduced in any form or by any means, electronic
or mechanical, including photocopying, recording,
or by any information storage and retrieval system,
without permission in writing from the publisher.

Printed in the United States of America

♾ This edition is printed on acid-free paper that
meets the American National Standards Institute
Z39.48 Standard.

Distributed in the United States by Random House, Inc.,
and in Canada by Random House of Canada Ltd

Library of Congress Cataloging-in-Publication Data
McClure, Michael.
    Touching the edge: dharma devotions from
    the hummingbird Sangha/Michael McClure
        p.   cm.
    ISBN 1-57062-440-2 (paper: alk. paper)
    1. Buddhist poetry, American.   I. Title.
PS3563.A262T6   1999   98-39898
811'.54—dc21   CIP

For the protection of all beings.

For Zenshin Ryufu, for Zentatsu, for Zoketsu.

For everyone in what Dogen calls "The Time-Being"
from Jane, Bill, James, and Michael,
to Shunryu Suzuki Roshi and Aitken Roshi.
For Gary and Carole Snyder and Hans and Pam Peeters,
and to the eagles they have shown us,
and also to the crickets
and deer on the hill.

With gratitude to Judith McBean Cosper

CONTENTS

NOTE

These dharma devotions may be seen and read like
calligraphy moving vertically on a white scroll.
They are almost as much for the eye as for the voice.
If the capitalizations and placement of lines seem strange,
then read them aloud and the ordinariness will appear.

rice roaring

———————

THE WHITE HAND WITH LONG FINGERS
HANGS OVER THE EDGE OF CONSCIOUSNESS
like a waterfall of peace.
Outside
a buck with velvet antlers
is stalked by a small
calico
cat.
E
V
E
R
Y
T
H
I
N
G
is flying apart
and
coming back
together
just
as it is.

Once I was all hormones
and energy,
WHOEVER

I
was

((am))

GOLD

WINDOWS

FIR BOUGHS

———

I WILL HAVE
A WHITE BEARD
and
white mustaches
like Manjushri
and a lion's
head will hang
in the air
and roar
by my shoulder
BUT
THAT
IS
NOTHING.
IT
IS
now
or
not.
My sword
will not chop down
the fuchsias
that hummingbirds drink from
but
only the mind's
CONSTRUCT
OF
REALMS

Nothing to stop
ME
now

IT
WILL
BE
THIS
way

it
will
be
that
WAY

NO TRACE OF REALIZATION
REMAINS
and it goes on and on
endlessly.
The great horned owls are gone
and the wind is here.
FOG
DECORATES
THE MORNING.
The bronze bell rings
through the branches
while
a green fig
rolls down the hill
by my foot.

Incense
makes
dragons
of
luck

I

IMAGINE

SEEING

THROUGH

((ALL))

THE
REALMS

and

they

are
not

there

JUST LITTLE FUNGI
looking
like
turkey tails
and
skid
marks
under
azaleas

GREED, HATRED, AND IGNORANCE
rise endlessly,
dumbly seeking
the Luminous.

OH
too old
to find it now,
it's
THERE
LIKE
A PIECE
OF CHOCOLATE
WEDDING CAKE
with dark frosting
reflecting
white roses

HOW MUCH I MISSED!

DON'T CHANGE ONE PULSE OF ONE GLAND!

— or
one
stealthy
sexual escapade

Dive through a billion
worlds of nasturtiums
and a billion wars
TO
STAY
NOBLE
AND
BRIGHT
where it is all o.k.
I
N

T
H
E

E
N
D

L
E
S
S
reflections
of nothingness

RUBBING MYSELF
through
all the universes
and realms
to
make
this
shape
and
NOT

EVEN

KNOWING
IT

is the Tathagata

as
are

the california poppies,
the golden yarrow
and the violet nightshade
by the burning incense.
Down through the rug
and under the floor
is
the
washing machine's rumble

and the cat's
disemboweled
baby junco.

IF
I
WAS A BOOK
I'D READ IT

I have full page
color illustrations
in sight, sound, taste, touch,
and smell,
to look beyond.
Now I close it. Now I open it

THE PASSIVE VOICE
ENCAPSULATES
PROTEIN
as
a
realm
does.
Flesh flares
and glows to cool
WHITE
from
organelles
with
smiling faces.
THOUGHTS
twine
around nothingness
reflected
in a lover's
blue eyes.

Tea and milk
float on the tongue
when drunk
from the cup
with
a
rooster
on
it.

Crusted dirt, hair,
dark flecks, are jewels
to no one.
No One
is here
with an orange
petal

and a gold ring

_____

EACH BREATH IS THE THOUGHT
that leaves
it

(or
not)

and the timid doe
watches me
from the intersection

while loquats ripen
in this world.

S
Q
U
I
R
R
E
L
S
run
over the roof.
It's all flying apart
and coming
together
as
fast
as
breath
and

jewel sand
grains
in
a
tidepool.

I'm a mountain?

Yes, and a bowl of rice
roaring

8

((CLEAR
    all
    clear.))

The great robe
of LIBERATION
is holes and holes
    in holes.
The fabric was used
    for caterpillars' dinners
        that grow
    moth wings
    with ten worlds
    of brightness
        on
        each
        drab scale.
Comme des Garçons
    sweaters,
        twisting
at each knot of the net,
        s
        m
        e
        l
        l
    of camphor
and Spring rain.
Cocaine in the nose
        and
    near air-crashes led
    TO THIS ELEGANCE
    to this beat surface
        glowing
        from nowhere
        with nothing.

            I'm
            glad
            you
            are
            here.

        I LOVE YOU.

Your
painted
toenails
are
abalone shells
in the morning light.

THIS

BUDDHA

LOOKS

LIKE

ME

THE LIMITATIONS
of imagination
are as
limitless
as imagination's
WAR
ON CONSCIOUSNESS.
Giant red honeysuckles
and collapsed dimensions
burst out of mountain boulders
in Peru
and in the parking lot
of the expensive market.
There's no warning,
it is all happening at once,
and
C
O
N
C
O
R
D
A
N
C
E
of these fantasies
is delusion
like the smell of halibut
sashimi
and the large scale
structures
of Time/Space.

Dragons of incense smoke.

Beards of dead friends.

THE DAY'S FANTASIES

ARE

SILVER PLATED

BY THIS BREATHING.

IT IS NOT SENSORY DEPRIVATION
BUT CONSCIOUSNESS-FULFILLMENT

TO
OBLITERATE

the
mind

for

ONE-TENTH

of a second

while
the blue-black jays
squawk
and
THE
BACK
forgets to ache.
One morning
a raven flies
over
making a q-u-a-r-r-k;
the next day I meet
a skunk on the street.
Her
pointed black nose
is as lovely as her plume of a tail.
I
can
pretend
I'm a hermit!

THE IMAGINATION IS NATURE.
Or is it?

Am I supposed to know?

(Lucky moths and hummingbirds.)

THIS

IS

ALL

I
EVER
WANTED TO BE

can be

will be

"THE CONTENT OF THE ENLIGHTENMENT"
is everywhere, nowhere.

HERE!

NOT HERE!

NO PLACE!

THERE,
in
the paralyzed hump
of the overweight woman
in the red dress
S
H
U
F
F
L
I
N
G
down the hill,
passed by cars,
pulled down by her
shopping bag.
The robin sings
on the wire
in the fog
IN
THIS
REALM

and

the

next

and

the

next

and in dimensions
within dimensions

BEING THE SAME

BEING DIFFERENT

LOOKING STRAIGHT AHEAD
INTO LOWERED EYELIDS
is as serious
as
a small mew
of
the calico cat
who
has
not
yet
caught
her
deer.
Violet deadly nightshade
and pale pink, thornless
roses
take on the odor
of incense
given
by friends.

G
A
R
B
A
G
E
TRUCKS
roar and grumble
and mulching machines
SCREAM
distressing the surface
of this infallible
B
O
D
Y

Darkness is darker
than it's ever been
before,
having
a
pleasant
weight

in the front
of
the

head

WELCOME, SPLASHED, SPLAYED,
and controlled and flailing ink
— I
can see my face
and feel my brain.
No stain is so much
that I may not
SMILE
ON
IT.
DARK SIDE
AND BRIGHT SIDE
WRIGGLE TOGETHER.
A
feather
wouldn't
say much more,
nor a trillion wise ones
making sweet medicine
for dying gods and mice.
IT'S
STRANGELY
DARK
INSIDE

b
u
t

not lonely

I
grow
deeper into
white
as black surrounds
me
and
hear imagined
echoes
of
imagined roaring

THE MIND WAVES
WRIGGLE AND INTRUDE
U
P
O
N
the center of nothing
which is
NETS
OF
NERVES
connected to nothing
and
quivering
and
vibrating
SUCH AS:
THE DEEP-CHESTED
WHITE EGRET
gliding above phone wires
at the foggy airport
AND
also
THERE
IS
THAT
WHICH

has
nothing

to
compare
it to

and no
language
to
speak
of it

((KNOW ALL THIS))

HOW?

THIS IS SURELY
A CAVERN
THAT
I
AM
PROJECTING

It has
jewels of tastes
and flowers
THAT
I'LL
never regret

I'M
THE FINAL
APOSTATE OF THE NOTHINGNESS
ILLUSION,

the Fantin-Latour
of the towering mauve
Jupiter's spear
in the altar bouquet,

W
O
N
D
E
R
I
N
G

when
the Morning Star
will
fill me
more clearly
more fully
than it does
in the dark
as
I look out
the bathroom
window.

Gray
paw

prints
on
the
black car.

———

THE SOUND OF THE AMTRAK
in the dark
of night
is
a stream
murmuring,
M
U
R
M
U
R
I
N
G.
I hear
it in fragments:
CHUNKS WITH EDGES
and silver and dark
sides
are a smooth rippling
flow.

JUST

AS

THERE

IS

graceful order
melting
into and out
of
nonpresence
before me and in me

IT'S A MOVIE
ON A WATERFALL
before me and in me
— nonpresence
melting
into and out
of
graceful order

Non-ghosts of nothing,
solid
as a baby's
love

———

MY HEAD PUSHES UP
INTO THE DARK CLOUD,
and buttocks
push down
into the cushion;
it's
the same
not knowing
and

T
H
U
S

C
O
M
E

once
again.
The rattle of tree
branches
blurs into
the wind
AS
THE
HUGE
BLOT
OF
THE
PLANE
drives over
the air.

None of it wasted.
None of it repeated.

"Hot
sun,
cool
breeze"

A CLOT
OF UNKNOWING
by
your
bare
foot.
Vimalakirti might
not approve
but
there are wars
and
roaring
in votive bouquets
like my head swarming
with dead friends and live
friends
and dreams.
The roar
that
is
not
there
is the power.
Manjushri's
beast
is more silent
than a swinging
SWORD
IN THE CAVE
OF
e
v
e
r
y
pleasure and pain.
Calligraphy, carving,
and poetry make
gods
that hang
around.

This is lovely
to be an
embodying.

THE SMELL IS BECOMING GOOD
and also present in my flesh
— cleanliness
is
S
U
M
M
O
N
E
D
FROM WHERE
DARKNESS
was before.
Tree roots
end at branch tips
in blossoms
and flowers
cankered by wasps.

BUT

THE

PERFUME

BRINGS

MOVIES

of forty years gone

which

TWITCH

AND SQUEAK

in
muscles
and hormones
of new practice.
Just one
s
m
i
l
e

at the trillion eyes and flashes
in darkness

((and deepness))

The surface of deepness.

"EXCESSIVE ACTIVITY"
like a mouse's heart.

There are
systems of sentient metabolism
convincing themselves
that they are five cats
in the gloaming
doing
a Noh dance
under the apple tree.
One
has a tail
like a fox

HOW

STILL

I

AM

FOR A MOMENT
— an uplifting
tripod
growing
a
center
of gravity
and not much else

L   L
I   I
S   S
T   T
E   E
N   N
I   I
N   N
G   G

won't get
me far

A

TINY

GRAY-WHITE

MOTH

IN A LIGHTNING FLASH
knows it all. (Imagine
the endless flash I live in
with green grass fields
of kalpas of dharmakayas, sentient odors
of Issey Miyake and Isamu Noguchi
carving granite into a dragon in a fresh
wind off Alcatraz.) A small bronze cup,
struck by a twig sprouting gray-green lichen
tings
sending me seeking the real

THE BIG REAL

D
E
E
P

I
N
S
I
D
E

me

OUT THERE

I'M
A
STRING
of disrelated pearls,
black with shadows,
WHITE
with the sun and moon
and frost patterns

EMPTY

ROARING IN A WATERFALL
where the bounce and slash
of the spattering drops

(icy,
harsh)

I
S

karma

or
not

OVER
and down
the stone slope
to where

your
hand

removes one
scarlet
oleander
blossom
making
the votive bouquet
more spacious,
perfect, transient.

Under the table
by the plug strip
the dharma cat
RAMPAGES
WITH
A
LARGE

crippled
fly

I want to paint a face
of Bodhidharma

QUALITY IS NO MIND BODY,
no body mind;

substance
is transiently part
of nothingness

OR
NOT

— being a hummingbird
asleep
in a thunderstorm
under
a ledge in the Andes

or

on
the phone
in New York City,
crashing among buildings;

and the smell, taste,
and touch of sitting upright,
with crossed legs, and the ring
OF
A
BELL

— by your side —

in
this

F
R
A
G
R
A
N
T
PRACTICE

THE QUALITY OF EMPTINESS
IS
NOT
STAINED,
but flickers
from moment-body
to mind-moment
in a solid froth
sitting
upright
with hooded eyes.
A soft bar of blurred light
hangs left to right
midway
in
my
forehead
resembling a painting
of great beauty
and deep meaning.
There are no edges,
only gradations
of subtlest colors interfering

WITH

THE FLIT

INTO NOTHINGNESS

returning as substance.

EVER
AND
EVER

is
nothing
maybe

THE YELLOW CAT
with the fox tail
is sleeping
curled in the sun
on
a
scatter
of deer shit.

M
O
R
N
I
N
G

F
O
G

arrives at night
to cover the full moon.
In the dream
I make Balinese
music
for Ray and Dorothy
with two color-encrusted
kazoos
and
tap
them together
for a glorious
crescendo.

IT'S

ALL

NOTHING

but

just what I've got,

right
now,
in the uncarved block

AT NIGHT
WHEN I STAND
IN THE FOG,
I cannot see it
against me.
A big owl feather
lies by the road,
it's invisible also.

Sipping sugar water
the hummingbird
squirts
milky fluid
on
the
deck.

Calmly
coming
into and out
of substantiality,
imagine
fog, or a red
hollyhock,
in front of the moon.
While squirrels
dash
over the roof

I

am

A

SILENT
TRIPOD

and

it's

ALL HAPPENING

SOMETIMES IT
is so calm
it is not there

e
x
c
e
p
t

for
the small
bell sound
like fur
turning to velvet

AND
STORIES

a
b
o
u
t

me

Bodhidharma's eyes
are wild and bloodshot
with rainstorms
and monsoons
and mountain forest ridges.
His cloak
is soaked and soggy
and he sits
by a big rock
STEAMING,
and
not
there.

Some
bamboo

———

There's always
CALM IN THE CENTER
o
f
DELUSION
— resting on
something else
surrounding it
while the calico cat snores.

NOT
MUCH

TO
KNOW

FOG FILLS THE TREES

STARS ABOVE

(out there)

R
A
C
C
O
O
N
S
have family quarrels
at the garbage cans

Delusion
resting on
REAL
insubstantiality

((or hunger
for organic
raisins
and green and
blushing apples

VAIROCHANA BUDDHA,
give peace, through
the long white fingers
of Kannon, to

O
U
R

friend
in distress.
I've never heard
of such flesh-carving
as she
endures; let
her slip easily
from realm to realm

and

LET

THE

MORPHINE

be a salmon

moving from stream
to ocean.

Apricots.

Blueberries.

The fur of her dog.

All
arise
around
her
as she moves
through them

THE THING THERE
is a memoir
of its own annihilation
— like the wine
that filled
a
ritual
bronze
vessel
that is now
blue and green
and flaking with oxidation.
It has a tiger head
that is almost
an
owl.

E
S
O
T
E
R
I
C
I
S
M
is not the point.
It's simple
as a cleanly sharpened
pencil or a paisley
bandanna seen
by
starlight
or soft
and crusted
mud
at the pond's edge.

I

WAS

WHOEVER.

BREATHE IN, BREATHE OUT,
INTO THE NOTHING.
— In between
is a tissue
of worlds,
with gods and kings and queens
and enzymes
and angers and laughters,
and they are swirled
into one
another
into
DEEPNESSES
BEYOND
DEEP

less

thick

than

a

white petal

or

a

color photo
of
August blackberries by the side
of the road.

Or sunlight on green leaves.

Semidarkness.

Smell of incense.

THE OVAL MUDRA
OF THE HANDS
is my breath,
holding a jewel.
It
is
all carved
where I sit.

Pictures of saints
painted on moving air.

BALD HEADS,
and calmed wild eyes,
say, "No,"
to dualism, to me
and something else.

I

W

A

S

W

R

O

N

G

IT IS NOT EVEN
one thing.

Bow to the night sky
inside of everywhere
and the morning star
that tastes like a fig.
Bow to your blue eyes
and soft toes;

we

might

die

but

we're being
born.

See where we are.

THIS IS EVERYTHING CHANGING
over and over
to be itself in me.
BUT
NOT
A
SHIFT
IN
SIGHT;
wisps and arms of fog
blow past the windows
by the big pine.
The cat's paws
are

a

fur
bouquet
as the bell *tings*.
Newborn mindfulness
becomes ordinary as black
cotton-covered cushions.
The mountain reaches
out to me
here
on the wooden bench
at the cliff edge.
Damp
blackberry jewels
are nets
of
Indra,
showing
the nonchanging
MUTUALLY ARISING

R
E
D
I
S
C
O
V
E
R
E
D

oval mudra

———————

TO GIVE IS THE WHITE HAND
with the long fingers
and the eye in the palm
P
U
T
T
I
N
G

FORTH
what is one,
already arisen,
and long gone.

The squawking of jays
is
a gift in the trees.

BE IN COMFORT CHET BAKER.

BE IN COMFORT JEAN-MICHEL BASQUIAT.

There are waves
and facets
and overlappings
and slidings
of
chunks
(and
non-chunks)
slipping
into
the ordinary

E
M
P
T
Y
roar
of the lion.
Plain
as
consciousness.

NOT THERE

GRAY-BLACK IN MY HEAD
and no hungers,
not seeing
the white lily
with stretching mauve petals
on the altar,
NO
SMELL
to the incense,
no vibration of the cat's purr:

IT

ALL

COMES

TOGETHER,

FLYING
APART.

QUIET
HERE.

NO
JAZZ
in the air

A
breeze
through the window screen.
Nothing crude
or gentle
or savage or silent.

JUST
THIS
THRONE
FOR
an instant

and soon sometime
another.
NOT THERE

THE WHITE CHIN OF THE FROG
        beats with his breathing.
            He's green
        and pinstriped
            — and as plain
                as I am;

                WE
            are naked
            and robed
                in
            the ordinary
                storm
                and
        waiting for rain.
        Not too smart,
            and not caring,
        we're wise apples.

                The
                F
                U
                L
                L

                M
                O
                O
                N

        makes a place
            to stand
        with raised arms.

            Next,
        I am brown-gold
        and old and wooden,
            solid,
        and near weightless,
        shaped like a buddha
                letting
                it
                go
        — or flash back
            to a few
        drops of rain
        on the windshield.

WE

DO
NOT

FEEL THE WAVES
in moony night, in fog,
inside
of
us,
with palms touched
together
and fingers pointed to sky
and then earth.

Samo,
samo,
to get to the river
and a little boat
in the rain
to cross it.

The roaring and thud
is heard
and not heard.

S
I
L
K

becomes shirts to cover
the shoulders
and waves flood out
to
robe
the sand.
WAVES RUFFLE
INTO

the
MIND
R
E
A
L
M

IT IS NOT THE SAME:
ALL REALMS ARE ONE

The sunset glow dissolves
  into the morning bell.
Confusing to nervous systems,
          N
          O
          T
          H
          I
          N
          G
      is everywhere
    in the whole thing.
      An incense finger
        trails over
      the quilt. Pelicans
    stream out in a flight
          above
          the surf.

          M
          O
          N
          K
          E
          Y

          M
          I
          N
          D

        thinks
    it knows some
        things
          and,
      in climbing,
        shakes

          the

        same

          old

      ladders

THE CHANGES CHANGE AND THOSE ARE CHANGIN

SEEN   then
ANY   those
DIRECTION   change

it is spreading

B
U
T
still
ONE

A tripod
breathing
on a black cushion
can embody
an edge
of a center

NOT
MUCH

just yellow fennel
at the roadside,
white mustard
with pink-tinted petals,
and wild poppies,
plain stuff

THE
PEACH
GOLD

v
i
b
r
a
n
c
y
of
the skin
of
your
arms.

Hot steaming water.
Nasturtiums.

THE CALICO KITTEN
is a cat now;
she basks on laps
A
N
D
stretches
enormous fingers and claws.
AVALOKITESHVARA
reaches out sinuous arms
from
the
tanka
newly discovered
behind the bookcase.
M
I
R
A
C
L
E
S

B
L
O
W

B
Y

as sizeless as clouds,
and car crashes
in Hollywood movies,
or the smell of a ripe
mango.
All things born have
shapes and timeless
histories

OR
NOT

Coming and going:
drips in painting

FOG IN THE TREES
is a miracle
and water falling over cliffs
is a fact.
The purple-black flower
is nothing
joining the act.
In the darkness
each dog bark
is a mudra
holding
a
circus.

IT
IS

PLAIN
AS

cartoons
in the daily paper

where armaments simmer
under the dollars.

ALL,

ALL

is
there
like rain on
a tree stump
or a worn-out work boot.
Imagine it shining
with the light
of the moment

and the voices
of children

FLEXIBLE MIND
flows over itself
admiring the details
and pliantly
forgetting.
The straight back
holds
everything
higher
than an anemone
growing above
redwood roots.

GREED

HATRED

and

IGNORANCE

rise

up

AT MIDNIGHT
like the morning.

Wisdom is calm readiness
buried under mildewed briefcases
and archives
of knowledge

B
E
C
A
U
S
E
the brain
will not
orchestrate
understanding,
a black branch
in front of the moon
is better.

THE MIND REALM IS IN BACK
of the mind
and unknown
to the thinker
making fabergé
puzzles
and structures.
Roller coasters turned
inside out
and backwards
MELT
on eyes,
ears, and nose.
Muscles
acting out
education
are
draped
with price tags
and
propaganda
WHILE
a
red and yellow apple
sits on a plate

I
HOLD
MY HANDS
like this: the thumbs
barely touching.

YOU
SOLID
GORGEOUS
GHOST,
perhaps this
is reason.

No,
too easy.

Just delusion.

———

A TINY YOUNG CRICKET'S
special nature
is presence
and nothingness,
hopping into the instant
and disappearing
in vibrancy
of hunger and winter
or
crawling

between old boards
of the deck floor.
S
T
A
R
S
and worlds
do no better
than *instars*.
Languages
have spotted fur
and are soft
to the touch.
Thorns of illusion
grow in the fur.
Beyond
the
barricade
we're
all the same.
Passing the wall
we're
ONE.
Pebble.
Stream.
Hangnail.

Scarlet snapdragon.
Motionless wine
in a moving flagon.

NINE MILLION LION THRONES
in this room
where I sit
on a black cushion
listening to my
monkey voice
A
N
D
it's all
O.K.

— AS

A

PLANE

ROARS

OVER,
the jays squawk
in cacophony
with it.
This
is real
as
things
get
on
this side
of dreams.

The nervous
system
is
very bright
very dark
and everything
else

Bundles
of sense impressions
in
constellation
and never
still
(like those imaginary
electrons)

THE CALICO CAT LIES
  on the high ledge
  in the darkness
  feeling
the huge space,
    blinking
    at light
  in the crack
  under the door.
  — IT'S JUST
  THE SAME
  WITH ME;
      I
  imagine
a shudder of pleasure
    and
  the sense
  of something
    beyond self
    filling emptiness
among cartons of old books,
    a stored
    vanity table,
and an antique sewing
    machine

  HOW

  PERFECT

  and

  MOMENTARY

  and

  ETERNAL

  Remember
pollywogs in cold
  spring ponds

  and

  their
  big

  dark eyes

REAL AS A FOREST STREAM
at night,
the sound pours
through
my
ears.
OLD
VOICES
in
strange languages
with accents
MAKE
LIGHT
AND
DARK
the same
they slip
them apart
into different faces
of the same
things
which are not
objects
or
coincidences.
LET
THIS

BE
A

LESSON,
it's a marriage
of illusions
like
ice cream
or
sleeping bags.
You
know
by touching it
with soft fingers
and fine
nails.

PICTURES AND STORIES
passing through
are no threat:
are "just illusion,"
says a patriarch.
"D
O
N'
T

W
A
S
T
E

T
I
M
E"
by not watching
them.

THEY
PROVE

I am here
in the dharma

made of boss stuff

((NON STUFF)).

Arrow points meet
in mid air
and
I'm
in the space
where they tap
and
everywhere.

Stories of money
and love
and intelligence
enacted
in bodies

and in pictures in bodies
are

not
there

?

———

THE SUBSTANCE OF EXPERIENCE
expands endlessly
in
flowers
and clouds
and smell of rubber
and sewage on
the freeway.
It
DEEPENS CEASELESSLY
as jewels are mined

from the Dharma

AND
COME

INTO
BEING

AROUND
IT.

I'M
LOST

ON
THE
WAY.

Casual pleasure. Mirth.
Risibility.

Five red-black button flowers,
three stems of purple
mexican sage and a large
white blossom with yellow center
hold the presence
of much
good odor

next
to
the candle.

WHAT I IMAGINE
resembles me
constricts
in
imagining.
Something
between in breath
and out-breathing,
a velvet curtain
of nerves
and habit,
IS
ME.

I
AM
IN
A
WORLD
WITHIN
WORLDS

— NEITHER FREE
NOR
not,
falling
like a yellow
leaf
in the wind
— and tasting like a raisin.

RAINDROPS
on windows
resemble
my thoughts

and

fingers

hold

hot tea

in

a

cup

with a painted rooster

THE POSTURE ITSELF IS THE SUBSTANCE
of
the search.
Compassion like crossed
legs may flow from the
MUDRA.
Thumb touches thumb,
back is straight,
and there's a dim screen
for the movies
that flock
to
the theater.
I
KNOW

ALL

EACH
TIME.

Raccoons screech
in the yard at night
and an early owl
is back
for autumn.
In the morning
a yellow-orange
harvest moon
rises
where the sun
should be
at sunset.

Jays mob
a sentient being
in the pine branches
and children
return
to the cracked rooms
and walls
of school

Posture

is

the substance

THE LEFT HAND IN THE RIGHT
and thumb tips faintly
touching,
begins in the toes,
neck, stomach,
and shoulders

M
A
K
I
N
G

a calligram
sitting upright.

I
REACH
OUT

AND
IN,

radiating
in numberless directions . . .

NOT
REALLY!

I'm here like
a jellyfish
or lion not

a quantum thing

or
a
fire
or a bolt
of zigzag lightning

Difficult to describe
HOW COMMON
this is

Crickets, frogs, snails
are all doing
this,
being
this

———

— DIFFICULT BEING HERE,
being my nature,
there's a thick shadow
of habits
D
I
R
E
C
T
I
N
G
THE SHOW.
In the canyon
the panicked
fawn
dashes ahead of the cars
too stunned
to dodge them.
What excessive grace
and freedom
in
her
pumping fearful
muscles.
HOW
ORDINARY
and
EXOTIC
the world is
You tap the bronze bowl
with a bent twig
crusted
with
gray lichen
and the realm
of
matter
is awash
and shimmered
by sound

SOMETIMES DISCONTENT
changes;
and nothing is gained
but
more of
the forgotten unknown
IS
FOUND.
Where it always
is:
RIGHT
HERE.
The touch of silk
answers questions
BUT
there is more
than the rustle,
the catch at a hangnail,
the smell of the moth
and the dyes
in the material.
NO
MIND,
NO
BODY.
(We are the fox
guarding the hen coop.)

IT
IS
ALL

SO RICH, SO GOOD,
SO PERFECT

—BUT

THE
PATTERNS
AND
SHAPES
are different
from what is imagined

I

AM

OLD
in the movie
but
this is real life;
wrinkles
drop away
with mind and body
and habits.

This

is

life

as a mudra
like
a porthole
in a storm.
Lion thrones
are carved
from
gems
of
no size.
This is all
provisional
providing
EVERY
POSSIBILITY.
I'm
MIDWAY
between carving
and writing
in the smoothing
and roughening
of life:
one side is laquered wood
the other is blank
paper

That's the cartoon.

DON'T ASK FOR THE BODY
it has gone
with the mind;
they are exactly equal
in weight.
They explore
for danger
and
there is none.
The orange melon
is blended
with yogurt
and honey
and
a
dash
of cinnamon
makes
an
adventure

of
landmines

and
uzis.

A carpenter
is hammering
poles
together
in the beatific silence.
U
T
T
E
R
LOVELINESS

(Machine saw roar)

LIKE A CREEPER
taking a flit
to the water bowl
for a quick
sip
that's all
I'm doing.
(A
year
of little
drinks.)

Trying
not to hold
onto anything
except the clay rim
and the wetness
of my beak
in the blare
of the heat
and yellow
leaves.
LET
LOOSE
OF
EVERYTHING
AND
also
the
ILLUSION
that I'm
holding
it.

I fly into
the autumn
branches
and cock
my dark eye
at the world.

When I speak
the bird doesn't
listen.
He's not
afraid.

ANOTHER MIRACLE.
A dying
dragonfly
on
the
asphalt.
Her body
is the tint
of a shimmering
green apple.

NOW

SHE'S HERE,

NOW GONE.

A
DHARMA

WITH
FOUR

STAINED GLASS
WINGS

Dregs
in
the
teacup
are
sunk
in
watery milk

B
O
D
H
I
D
H
A
R
M
A
moves to the east
and the ship
rocks

ONLY THE THIRD RING
of the bell
is heard
through the cloud
of delusion
and amusing
fantasy

The
H
U
M
M
I
N
G
B
I
R
D
hears nothing
and floats
like a boat
in the sound.
A HUGE EGO
laden with attachments
is hunting
my mind
as waves crash
on this body.

HOW
FAR

IS

IT

TO
the other side?

How many smells
are left
to smell?

How many peaches
still to eat?

THE STICK GLANCES AND SLIDES

over the bell
but
the ring
is pure
and shimmers
as ever.
I
AM
THE
PROBLEM
but I'm not
an answer
The rose-breasted nuthatch
is no longer
afraid
and he drinks
from the waterbowl
as I stand
watching
and tapping
the bell.
Mystical
calligraphy is made
by the slide of raw
cabbage
as it rubs
through
the
salt
on the black plate.

EVERYTHING

IS

EVERYTHING

ELSE

THE CONTENT OF ENLIGHTENMENT
is hummingbirds
W
H
I
R
R
I
N
G
through clouds
of butterflies
between the branches
of the morning glory tree
and the crashing
of big mobile
machines
drilling holes
for
new
telephone poles.
This I am
sure of in
record
heat
as leaves fall
flatly
to the earth.

Listening One,
hear the griefs
of the salamanders
whose skins
crack in this weather.

Bring
mercy
to those
who are butchered
in
the
abattoirs
of ignorance
and
hatred

———

IN THIS WORLD
the problems seep
into me

WHEN
THERE

ARE

silver
stars

on black velvet;
this is followed by
brown fog
and
auto sounds.
All that
is
one sub-quark
of reality
ON
THE
BIG
SCREEN
OF
the
REALMS
where
I
doubt
at the center.

Roses grow
near gardenias

AND
YOU

sit next to me.

EACH
DAY

is a mudra
and a calligram

THE OLD BRONZE BELL
RINGS
and the spiderweb
shimmers
in morning sunlight.
It is all gone,
Beauteous One,
gone
on
the
boat
to the other shore
though it rests,
like my hands,
on my lap.
It's
L
O
V
E
L
Y
as a poem
in the voice
of Anakreon:
paced and shaped
and singing
like
a bee rustling
among
petaled
treasures
or
Manjushri's
snow lion
roaring
as
the sword

SWINGS

to chop out
the walls
between
realms.

A SHADOW
of enlightenment
feels like pleasant
madness;
in
a
fantasy
it ripples
from the other shore
up through the stomach
and chest.
IT'S
NOTHING,

NO
FEAR,

SVAHA.

JAYS
CLUCK

in the falling
of leaves

There's a baby
green cricket
in the apple tree.

T
H
I
S

I
S

A
L
L

S
O

ORDINARY,

plain
as a walnut

RESIDUAL FEAR
of enlightenment
lies
in the muscles
like leftover adrenaline.
(I
NEVER
WORRY
ABOUT
THAT.)
Everything is the color
of all colors:
airplane engines
passing
over
and blue quilts
beneath.
Small soft mountains
of mist
cover the trees
and ooze
into the canyon.

KEEP QUIET
and feel Bodhidharma's
comments
on the Precepts.
WE
HAVE
gone
TO
the
OTHER
side
by being here.

This is the other bank
all
day
long
AND
at night
there are light bulbs
and beeswax
candles

THERE'S NO FEAR OF KNOWING
or not knowing.
Bits of fact
about the evolution
of eagles
and pains in the knees
are knots
in a web that shivers
C
A
T
C
H
I
N
G
experiences.
The window
of mind
breathes through my stomach
in a mudra
like a baby bobcat
licking its fur
in the sunlight.
There is a black stone
with white veins
under the oak tree
and rough bark covered
with lichen
lies scattered
in dry grass

New bookcases and curtains
are eternal
many times
in a moment.

THIS IS SOLID

MULTIFACETED

AND
FLOWING

in several directions.

It's a persimmon.

wet plank

———

THE WHITE HANDS WITH LONG FINGERS
hold an injured ego,
touching its thorns,
caressing the lids
of its bloodshot eyes.
REALMS
open
and close
in a
tidepool.
C
L
E
A
R
cold
water
streams from a vial
and every night
is a new night.

The *thrummm*
and glitter
of the hummingbird
comes from nowhere
and the doe
steps awkwardly
to look at
the calico cat.
Sunrise
is
N
O
T
H
I
N
G
but
pink-orange,
abalone-patterned
scatterings
of
clouds

MONKEY MIND BUILDS CATHEDRALS
of imagination and stone
and tone poems
of stained glass
and bubblegum.
I inhabit
C
I
V
I
L
I
Z
A
T
I
O
N
like a plump cricket
or a dust mote
in an empty mansion
and listen for the garbageman
who plays jazz
with his truck.

THIS

IS

SO

EASY

and I create problems
with it:

fighter bombers,
mutilations,
epiphanies of envy,
ALL
WHEN
I
MIGHT

be nestling
in comfort and ease.

EACH RAINDROP IS AN INSTANT
in birth
as everything
changes.

WE

ARE

IN

MIST

and

we

glance
toward the forest.

Now
your
foot
is
ivory
on the blue quilt
by the round, black
cushion;
it is cool
and electricity
pops the lights
in the storm.
Perhaps
N
I
R
V
A
N
A
is
ceaseless change
in muscles and voices.

As glib as a lily
or a lightning bolt.

I

WILL

NOT

do this again.
I am waves
of material
and everything else.
Hormones whispered
to by patriarchs
are moving
IN
THE
RAIN.
I am raining
and loud
with downpour
and
there are silences
between each drop

I

trickle

through the walls
of the basement
and across the concrete
floor.

THIS

IS

EITHER

A PERSIMMON

OR

A PINECONE.

Or something else?

THE NEWS NEVER CHANGES.
The big picture is there
and the eyes, ears, nose,
skin, and tongue twist
to become
an apple or velvet.
The jelly mass
in the spring pond
flowers into pollywogs
wriggling for tasty
algae
— and the presence
of salty surf
on the ankles and calves
is a statue
of neurons.
In the mirror
streams flow
to the waterfall
and
Manjushri's snow lion
coughs
in a jeweled grotto
as the flame sword
swings.

Turtles
have
good
dreams
sleeping
in
the mud
though
we
will
never

meet
them.

I GO DEEPER

INTO
THE FUTURE

I
MAKE

BEAUTEOUS ONE, GIVE ME
one drop of wisdom
now that I have one.
The future is lace
on the hem
of compassion,
it
is there
to decorate
the streams in the mirror
that
write
out
the sky's
story.

Make this easy
as warm arms
and smooth skin
that
fill
one
with nothing.

Let this small house
sing
in the wilderness
and
allow beings
to
feast
here
in the memory
of friends.
Many have gone
and we meet them
in thoughts
and
dreams
and faces
around us.

WITH SOFT FLEXIBLE MIND,
I am here forty years
ago
and have tender
eyes
and no wrinkles.
B
E
I
N
G
young

IS PAINFUL
and

not
free

and movement
is quick honey.

This is movie,
and counter-movie,
reflected
through kaleidoscopes

ONTO
BLACK MERCURY

MAKING

ME

exactly

this
way.

I
sit
smiling
with pleasure
in
delusion

THE SHAPE OF MY THOUGHTS,
filled with projects
of words,
discovers energies.
I
AM
THIS

I

AM

THAT

Small sentences
reward
silence
while
two raccoons
with masked faces
leer
from a storm drain

BROWN
LEAVES

flutter
onto red brick.

There is no prize
for this
and no cause
except
its
reflected arising
where once
there was glowing
and nightmares.

Now
times

have
other
shapes

NOTHINGNESS GIVES RISE TO ME
and to breathing
as car sounds
spread
through air paths
of hummingbirds.
A huge
PLANE
passes over
THE REALM
of
cancer
and youth and age
and sashimi
and ripe peaches.
Friends
grow ill
or
receive
prizes

AND

THE FULL MOON
is smaller
at sunrise.

Midnight has
falling leaves
haloed with light
and silver
spider webs.
THIS

is

ALL
NEWS

to emptiness

JUST
AS
I
AM

MOVIES OUT THERE
in dark caves
with crashing sounds
and soft seats
D
I
S
T
O
R
T
the fragments
of dramas inside.
The actors are tiny
and slender
and urgent.
ELSEWHERE
are behemoth
and sizeless
imaginings
of the crude oil
and ivory
of extinction
where the stadium
is carved from
NOTHINGNESS.

THIS
IS
NOT
POSSIBLE
TO
THINK
ABOUT,
for which
I am grateful

as the calico cat
slides
over the linoleum
chasing
a cork
with her tail fur
on end.

THE MOMENT OF EMOTIONAL PASSION
is flame swirling out of childhood.
All the hot tears
and red cheeks
can be shaped
into readiness
of mind.
JEALOUSY
and
ANGER
are
windows.
The bell's
third ring
sounds
through clouds
while
the hummingbird
sips
from the white
trumpet
that peeps from purple
wrappings.

Odor
of
I
N
C
E
N
S
E,
and friendly
voices,
hang in the room
and I know
them

again

and let gratitude
replace fear

_____

A PATRIARCH SAYS THERE IS NO BUDDHA
without living beings.
We are appearances
of nothing
that
shiver
in no breeze
and are
as present
and solid
AS
rocks
carved into frogs,
and black skillets.

WHAT
I
PRACTICE
FOR

IS
HERE

before I wish it.

ALERTNESS
not
experience
is
wisdom.

I

HAVE

O
N
E

T
O
E

on the wet plank
of a little boat

THE SCARLET-HEADED WOODPECKER
feels no shame
and is gone in a moment

JUST
AS
I
AM.
There's no hole
or space
left behind

HE'S
GONE.

I'M
GONE

like a bell ring.

The bell
is no smaller
there is no diminishment.
The rings are richer
as the bronze
turns green

The

cat

finds

a

universe

under

each

leaf

in the yard

AND
MANJUSHRI'S LION
ROARS.

REXROTH BELIEVES EVERYTHING
might be sacred
if we allow it.
I hear
that enlightenment

must
precede

PRACTICE,

NO
SENSE
in striving
for the ideal

WHEN

lion thrones
are everywhere.

The cold mist
out there
makes
the heater
whir here.

Final
yellow leaves
hang
on thin branches
over
the edge
of the old
dock,
wavery with
water grass
and studded
and engraved
with
GOLD
and
dark
lapis
lazuli

STUDY OF SELF PEELS OFF
the known self:
body and mind
drop
A
W
A
Y
from the upright
tripod.
Leaf by leaf
the tree brushing the deck
strips
to
its
dark
trunk
and slender
branches.

NEXT
THERE

w
i
l
l

BE
PUSSYWILLOWS
in a canyon
at the edge

OF

THE

OCEAN.

Gray fur blossoms
the size of a thumb

gather
COLD
POINTS

of wave mist.

THE PARADE GOES ON
with red wagons
and steam calliopes
pulling carts with screens
showing
M
O
V
I
E
S;
I am the cruel victor,
the hero, the victim,
the monster.
SOMETIMES
there is a slippage
of patterns
forming myths
as thin
as knife blades,
through muscle
bundles.

NOW

IT

ALL

GIVES
WAY

TO

LARGENESS

THAT I RECOGNIZE

FOR

THE FIRST

TIME

CALM MAKES A FRAME
FOR THE LURID;
the bright purple
and red splashed on
shining green
silk
i
s
PRECIOUS.
The prayer flag
of Bodhidharma's face
is motionless
over the door
on a windless day.

His portrait
is black and white
and his eyes bulge
and the heart beats
in his big chest.

An old chunk
of oak bark
is overgrown
with gray-green
and orange lichen
and
it
rests
on the gray rock
ready to sleep
(or poised to pounce
out
of
this world.)

Taste of vanilla
in the mouth
and odor
of costly incense
in the air.

Does ignorance
lead to this?

EXPERIENCE IS WEIGHTLESS;
philosophy is a lead lifejacket
decorated
with bright bubbles.
I
SWIM
through this practice
without motion.
OLD
WORDS
ancient
words,

drop
their meaning

AS

THEY

SOUND

IN
ME

IN DARK
OF MORNING.

Deepness and richness
are nothing

and
crickets

are
alive

and chirping
in the chilly dawn.

Orion's belt
is three stars
on the other side
of the roof.

NOT TO THINK OF BUDDHA
   is the center of sitting
    and bowing
 — as empty as a flower
     in wind.
       D
       E
       E
       R

       S
       L
       E
       E
       P

   in matted grass
   under an oak
   on the ridge
     as
   thoughtless
    and
   thoughtful
     as
 a passenger plane
  or red yo-yo.

  Frank's chest
    heals
  where the heart
  was laid open.
    HE
   WAITS
    TO
  RETURN
   HOME
  to the trees
  and his waterfall.
    He
   says,
"I'm in love with nature,
   I guess."

BE IN COMFORT, FREEWHEELIN FRANK

  (BE DEEP AS YOU ARE,
   OLD HERMIT)

THE CLEAR CENTER IS PRESENT.
Now I am here.
Now elsewhere.
THE HOUR OF THE WOLF

b
r
i
n
g
s

CONFUSION
to flurry
at the mirror
WHAT PLEASURE
to eat oatmeal
with green apple, raisins,
and honey from New Zealand

CHAIN
SAWS

hack
at trees.

The rainstorm is coming
on wings of TV

Nothing is different.
NOTHING THE SAME.

THE

CALICO

CAT

LEAVES

gray footprints

on
the round, black
cushion.

I MAKE MY CENTER IN DELUSION.
Enlightenment is the color and taste
of life.
The feel of blue denim,
smell
of wool
and sound of the chain saw
are the tanka
of circumstance.

THIS

IS

PROOF
of freedom

LIKE
AN OLD
BUCKET

half full of water

IGNORANCE
is a crutch
for
me

just
as

your blue eyes
and hands are

LET
ME
BE
cheerful
and modest

as I peer
from this refuge.

THERE ARE THREE THINGS
to remember
and
they
are gone with the waterfall

I
AM

where I always
am.

A
WINDOW
of
flesh
looks through
illusion.

A SMILING EGO
coils
R
O
U
N
D
the mirror.

It is lifted down

AND
HELD

IN
SOFT

ARMS

and placed in the boat.
Waves slosh the sides.
Rocks scrape the bottom.

Baby catfish
dart in the shallows
brushing pebbles
with their whiskers

A SMALL INSECT CRIPPLEDLY HOBBLES
in sunlight over the box top,
LEGS SHAKING AND STUMBLING.

WHAT
THINGS

he knows
of himself.
Unmeasured rooms
of the self
meet in him.
VAST
HALLS
come together
mirroring the flicker
of nothing.
Probably there are no
ideals there
nor
imaginings
of light in a snow lion's
eye.

The flame-sword swings
AND
EMPTINESS
OF
WISDOM

r
o
a
r
s

like a stomach
on fire with garlic

There can be
no buddha
without beings.

THE SMELL OF MORNING INCENSE
lights up
a memory
of the thrown rod in the car.

O
U
T
S
I
D
E

is luminous sunlight,
and wind
shaking the trees,
into flickers and flashes.

I
N
S
I
D
E,

all things
join hands
as I am torn away
from the empty river.

This might be real
as a new atlas,
dusty black shoes,
or
grime on a paint job

LET
ME

(*Svaha!*)

HAVE

(*Svaha!*)

quiet courage

DESPITE FASCINATION
DO NOT BE CONCERNED
that form is emptiness
and emptiness is form.
IT
IS
ALL
a brown
falling leaf
no different from
anything
else.

NOT
PLAIN

NOT
BRIGHT

(perhaps)
mysteriously
elegant.

OWLS
ARE
BACK

courting
in darkness
with their firm
and unsure voices.

THE
CAT'S
WHITE PAWS
catch
a
last
butterfly.

When alert and unfocused,
traffic
is the sound
of the world.

NOR DOES KNOWLEDGE CHANGE
the mist in front
of looming trees
ON
A
COOL
MORNING
with robins
chirping
and
rose blossoms
dying.

Something
is the beeping
of trucks
and an ageless
river.

Something
is a rug and a candle
and a boat
with no name.

Something
is
empty;
nothing
is
full.

Pink, curled petals
drop from the rose
as
it
shakes.

This
is
the purple
mexican sage
that
I pick
for the altar.

THE PINK OF DAWN IS GONE
in
T
U
R
M
O
I
L.

Through your eyes,
your shoulders,
Amoghapasha-Lokeshvara
brings surcease.
His eight strong arms
are in you
as you breathe on me.
His nectar and sutra
bring ease.
Your shoulders are his rope
pulling me to dharma.

THE TASTE OF DELUSION
is turkish delight.
HOW
WE
LOVE
TO
FEAST
on it
as it falls
through the mirror
to the other side.

We
lie

in
the sheets
laughing and sweetened
with precognition
of a grain of wisdom

See the trident
and rosary.

— A LITTLE NAKED OF EGO
for a moment
like
taking clothes off.
Lightness through the body
and easy footed;
being here
IS
ONE
WAY
TO BE
in the changing mix
of music.

THE HEAVY WORLD
is
pliant

plain

SOLID
and
WEIGHTLESS.

The three treasures
surround me.
R
E
F
U
G
E
is
the alert pigeon
peering at the sky
through smog
from the hotel roof.

Contained
as thick green tea
in a white cup.

A DOE CROSSING THE STREET
waits
in mist
for her yearling fawn.
Mother and daughter chew ivy
from the trunk
of a pine.
Wet stars fall
on their backs.
RAIN
COMES
in looming sun.

The old black car
waits
in the repair shop

I

AM STRENGTHENED

by my art
and those
who love me

and teach me

THIS

MAY BE

D
E
L
U
S
I
O
N

but it shines

EMPTINESS IS FORM
and therefore
enlightenment;
I

SURELY

KNOW

what I practice

FOR.

B
E
F
O
R
E
dawn
I stop for
an elegant
skunk
in the glen.
WE DANCE
forward and back
on the street
and I
pass her
while she snoops
in the storm drain.
What
GORGEOUS
LOVELINESS
in the cracks

and

the crevices

of
the twirlings
and the blinkings
of stuff

(This is serious)

CAN I KNOW EMPTINESS
by touching the calico fur
of the cat?
Black,
white, brown, yellow-orange,
pink paw-pads,
and the sound of her purr,
are
SCULPTURE
on a flickering
banner
that flies
on a boat made
of odors and sounds
of helicopters
and cinnamon
incense?

Can
I ransack
the drawers
of the realms
to
understand
NOTHING?

Will
C
O
M
P
A
S
S
I
O
N
speak
to
me?

It's so easy
that it's not easy

SILENCE IS A ROAR
with white hands.
NOISE
is born out
of it
distracting me
with the purple arms
of mexican sage.

Sun
slips into this realm
with a psychedelic flash.
I
find a grain
of compassion
and its polished surface
mirrors my face.
THIS
IS
ME
AS
I AM.

SEE
MY
EYES
AND
MY NOSE
and my mouth

ME

AS

I
AM

reflected from pearl
to pearl
in the crown

DARK PATHS ARE THE WAY
to the light
in
the
forest
where the mountain gleams
after rain
and thunder.
S
E
L
F
KNOWLEDGE
flashes like sun
in a downpour.
A
milligram
is
PURE
GOLD
wrapped in actions
and carried to the old boat.
The rustlings of leaves
in the yard are songs
of clarity
praising the changing
of forms.

We are the touch of silk
and taste of peaches and steamed beets.

HOW SOLID AND EMPTY.

HOW

SOLID

AND

EMPTY

IS

THIS

DHARMA

Postscript

Devotion 2 is for Anne Waldman and Andrew Schelling,
who breathed incense on us.

Devotion 4 is for Zoketsu Norman Fischer,
who performed our wedding.

Devotion 36 is for Shunryu Suzuki Roshi,
who is a frog and a waterfall.

Devotion 51 is for Zenshin Ryufu Philip Whalen,
who read zen poems to me in 1955.

Devotion 57 is for Edward and Miriam Sanders,
who know the birds.

Devotion 66 is for Hans and Pam Peeters,
who give the wildness of California.

Devotion 70 is either a persimmon or a pinecone,
for Diane di Prima and Shepard Powell.

Devotion 76 is for Francesco Clemente,
who said he wanted it.

Devotion 89 is for Zentatsu Baker Roshi,
who first invited me into the Sangha.

ABOUT THE POET

Michael McClure has been an essential member of the Beat literary movement from its beginnings. In 1955, at the age of twenty-two, he joined Allen Ginsberg, Gary Snyder, and Philip Whalen at the legendary 6 Gallery in San Francisco where Ginsberg first recited *Howl*. Today he continues to be influential in the poetry scene, performing his work in venues as varied as the Fillmore Auditorium, Yale University, and the Library of Congress. The *Poetry Flash* described one of his readings: "McClure—dressed in black—stood and uttered his words with a sort of sultry precision. His gestures punctuated his words (a poetry of the body), enthralling, enlisting a dynamic tension between audience and performer that didn't let up until the words stopped."

In the early 1990s Michael McClure began performing his poetry with music by his old friend, the keyboardist and composer Ray Manzarek. Mystic Fire Video has released *Love Lion*, a video tape of one of their performances, and their CD *Love Lion* was recorded at the Bottom Line in New York. *Third Mind*, a documentary film about the collaboration, was premiered at the Los Angeles County Museum in 1998.

The poet's seventeen books of verse include *Dark Brown, Jaguar Skies, September Blackberries, Selected Poems, Rebel Lions*, and the recent *Simple Eyes*. McClure is also the author of more than twenty plays and musicals, two novels, and three collections of essays. In collaboration, he has written the autobiography of a Hell's Angel friend and worked in the fine arts field with Bruce Conner, Wallace Berman, and Robert Graham.

His journalism has appeared in *Vanity Fair*, the *Los Angeles Times*, and *Rolling Stone*.

Michael McClure lives with his wife, the sculptor Amy Evans McClure, in the Bay Area.

Visit Michael McClure's web page at

http://www.thing.net/~grist/l&d/mcclure/mcclure.htm

COVER ART

The Great Bodhisattva One Hand by Torei. The calligraphy begins with the One Hand itself, followed by the Chinese character *Dai* or Great. This character is written oddly to make it look like a stand or pedestal, also *Dai*. The calligraphy is in the *myogo* style, the usual formula for which is: "Homage to such-and-such a Buddha or Bodhisattva." Often this type of calligraphy would be hung behind a Buddhist altar—equivalent to placing it on a pedestal there). Characters three and four are *Bosatsu*: Bodhisattva. Hence the calligraphy can be read "the Great Bodhisattva One Hand" or "the One Hand itself being the Bodhisattva."

Printed in the United States
by Baker & Taylor Publisher Services